pug

understanding and
caring for your dog

Written by
Ellen Williams

pug

understanding and
caring for your dog

Written by
Ellen Williams

Pet Book Publishing Company

Bishton Farm, Bishton Lane, Chepstow, NP16 7LG, United Kingdom.
881 Harmony Road, Unit A, Eatonton, GA31024 United States of America.

Printed and bound in China through Printworks International.

ISBN: 978-1-906305-70-3
ISBN: 1-906305-70-6

Acknowledgements

The publishers would like to thank the following for help with
photography: Jan Foster, Daphne Crump (Pigalle),
Elaine Passmore (Pelancy), Jason Hunt (Carpaccio),
Sabine Stuewer (www.stuewer-tierfoto.de).

Contents

Introducing the Pug

The Pug is one of the most distinctive looking of all our breeds, and it is rare indeed to get a case of mistaken identity. The breed motto is *multum in parvo* – "much in little" – which means you get a lot of dog in a little body.

The Pug is small and compact, but his proportions are square and cobby, so you get the impression of a substantial little dog. But the motto, *multum in parvo*, rings out most truly when it comes to temperament. The Pug is big on personality – a charming mixture of dignity and playfulness combined with the most loyal and loving disposition.

Physical characteristics

The Pug is a Toy breed and fits comfortably on a lap or a sofa, but his well-knit proportions and muscular build allows him to live the life of an active dog.

The Pug's most distinctive feature is his round head, with its short muzzle, flattened nose, and small, velvety ears. The eyes are round and dark, with a melting, lustrous expression which become bright and full of fire when he is excited. The typical furrowed brow, created by the wrinkles on the forehead, can also make him look serious and thoughtful.

The Pug can be all shades of fawn, ranging from silver through to apricot, or pure black. Fawn dogs have black markings, which should be well defined.

When he moves, the Pug has a steady and purposeful stride; a slight, unexaggerated roll of the hindquarters is a breed speciality.

Brachycephalic breeds

The Pug is classed as one of the brachycephalic breeds, a group of dogs that share a particular type of head construction.

The smaller brachycephalic breeds include the French Bulldog, the Pekingese, the Boston Terrier and the Shih Tzu. The bigger breeds include the Boxer, the Bulldog, and the Dogue de Bordeaux. You may not think these breeds look very much alike, but they all have a broad, short skull, with a foreshortened muzzle and a pushed-back nose.

These features should be distinctive, but never exaggerated, as this type of conformation can result in labored breathing, particularly in hot weather.

It also accounts for another Pug speciality – this is a breed that snores! However, most owners find the snuffles and snores of a sleeping Pug most endearing; just one of the many features of owning this highly distinctive breed.

Pictured: Despite their difference in size, the brachycephalic breeds – Shih Tzu (left) and Dogue de Bordeaux – share a similar head structure.

Temperament

The Pug is a friendly, confident dog, and likes nothing better than to be with his beloved family. His aim in life is to please – and to entertain – and he will be most put out if he is excluded from family activities.

There is no doubting his intelligence; this is a dog that will work things out when it is to his advantage, but he may not always be so co-operative in fitting in with your plans. Some say the Pug has a stubborn streak, but it is more a matter of knowing his own mind and being unwilling to compromise.

The clever owner who understands the Pug brain soon becomes skilled in cajoling a Pug into thinking that something is his idea – and then he will be only too happy to do as you ask!

A dog for all

The Pug is small, robust and adaptable and, as a result, he will fit in with most family situations. Town or country, family home or apartment, he will be happy as long as he is with his people. He is better suited to living with children than some of the daintier Toy breeds, and his playful disposition and sense of fun will make him a most entertaining companion.

Facing page: The gentles snores of the Pug are a breed characteristic.

His short coat is easy to care for and, as far as exercise is concerned, he will fit in with what is available. He is more than capable of going for a long, rambling trek in the country, but if his owners are getting on in years, he will make do with pottering around in the garden.

However if his exercise is limited, it is important to provide sufficient mental stimulation – and to keep an eye on his waistline.

Living with other animals

The Pug is a very sociable dog and will enjoy the company of other dogs – particularly his own kind. Pugs are one of those breeds that seem to be highly collectable, so watch out – before you know it, your numbers may grow.

If you own a larger breed of dog, there is no need to worry as the Pug will look after himself. He has a self-assured, dignified character which puts others dogs in their place, and he is tough enough to play with a bigger dog as long as the game is not too boisterous.

Facing page: The Pug enjoys the opportunity to use his brain.

The family cat has nothing to fear, as long as initial interactions are carefully supervised. In fact, there are some Pugs that have formed a very special friendship with their feline housemates, and positively enjoy curling up with a cat.

The Pug does not have a strong prey drive, but if you keep small animals, such as hamsters or guinea pigs, they should be housed securely and, even so, your Pug should never be left alone with them. It is far better to be safe than sorry.

Life expectancy

We are fortunate that, in common with many Toy breeds, the Pug has a good life expectancy and should reach 12 to 14 years of age. In fact, many Pugs survive into their mid teens.

Tracing back in time

The Pug has an ancient history, and has claims to being one of the oldest dog breeds in the world. His roots are in China, and there are Chinese documents describing short-nosed dogs that bear a strong resemblance to the Pug dating back to 700BC.

It is not until 100AD that we get further evidence of Pug-like dogs. This centers on the Szuchuan province of China where there are records of four short-faced breeds:

- The Chinese Pug, known as the Lo-tze: A small fawn dog with black markings.

- The Chinese Mastiff: A larger fawn dog, with black markings, possibly sharing common ancestry with the Lo-tze.

- The Pekingese: A small dog coming in a variety of colors.

- The Japanese Spaniel: Also coming in mixed colors.

It is thought that the Pekingese and the Japanese Spaniel evolved later, starting as long-nosed breeds and being selectively bred over a period of time to conform to the fashion for short-nosed breeds.

The Chinese Pug, or Lo-tze, was singled out for special attention by the Chinese emperor. A law was passed stating the Lo-tze could only be owned by the emperor; illegal ownership was punishable by death. The emperor's dogs were kept in the royal palace, living in their own special quarters. They were attended to by their own servants and were guarded by soldiers. Emperor Ling (168-190 AD) even gave his favorites royal titles – the females shared the same rank as his wives.

Wider recognition

The Lo-tze was not known outside China until an overland trade route was established to the West. As well as silks, and other expensive commodities, some highly prized Lo-tze made the journey. In AD 732 a Lo-tze was sent from Korea as a gift to the Japanese Emperor.

Over the next 200 years, there is a spattering of reports of Lo-tze outside China. Interestingly, different colors were described, including black, so this may be the origin of our black-colored Pugs.

China then went into a period of isolation, so there is no further news of the Lo-tze until a sea trade was established between Portugal, Spain and Canton in 1516. The little dogs from China soon became favorites of the aristocracy, and were referred to

in court circles as 'Isabellan', which was the name
used for their fawn-colored coats.

The dutch connection

The Netherlands was to be become highly influential
in the story of the Pug – and it was all because of a
timely, warning bark!

In the 16th century, the Netherlands was ruled
by Spain and, led by William I, Prince of Orange,
the country was battling for independence.
William owned a Pug, named Pompey, possibly
obtained from the Spanish court, and the little dog
accompanied him everywhere.

In the dead of night, a party of assassins approached
William's tent but, fortunately, Pompey heard them
coming. He gave a warning bark, which was enough
to awaken his master so he could escape to safety.
From that moment onwards, the Pug was adopted by
the House of Orange.

The Dutch finally gained independence, and in 1602
they established their own trade with China, through
the Dutch East India Company. This connection
meant that more Pugs found their way to Europe,
and when William and Mary of Orange acceded to
the British throne in 1689, their beloved Pugs came
with them.

The diminutive Pug, also known as the Dutch Mastiff because of its marked resemblance to the mighty English Mastiff, remained a royal favorite in the centuries that followed, and during Queen Victoria's reign (1837-1901) the Pug became the most popular Toy dog in the UK.

Pictured:
Spot the likeness:
The Pug was thought
to bear a strong
resemblance to the
English Mastiff.

Developing the breed

While the Pug was reaching new heights of popularity in the UK, it was also becoming well established on the other side of the Atlantic. The first Pug was registered with the American Kennel Club in 1885, and the first American Champion was Ch. George, bred by Leila Tregvan of South Carolina, who imported a bitch in whelp from the UK.

From the early 20th century onwards there was an increasing number of imports, mostly from the UK. American enthusiasts were prepared to pay high prices; in 1900 Mrs Gould, a New York Pug fancier, paid $500 for Black Knight and Canonbury Princess, which were exorbitant prices for the day.

The most influential breeder in these early days was Al Eberhardt from Ohio, who imported Finsbury and Haughty from the UK, and went on to establish a line of successful show dogs in the USA.

What's in a name?

The Pug's unique expression, with his serious-looking furrowed brow, earned him a different name in Europe. In Sweden he is known as Mops, in Germany and Holland he is called a Mops Hond, and in Finland he goes by the name of Mopsi.

These names derive from the Dutch word 'mops', meaning 'to mope', clearly referring to the Pug's doleful expression.

Black pugs

Although there were early records of black Pugs, it was the fawn-colored Pugs that found favour in Europe and the USA. Black Pugs may have disappeared altogether had it not been for the dedication of Lady Brassey, a noted breeder of the Victorian era. She had a passion for black Pugs, and was determined to establish a breeding line of top-quality dogs.

She often traveled to the Far East on the family yacht, and it is likely that she brought dogs back from China with her. She exhibited her Pugs in the show ring, and at the Maidstone Show, in 1886, she owned all the entrants!

She worked tirelessly to promote the color, and although fawn Pugs still dominate the show ring, black Pugs have a devoted worldwide following.

The modern era

The Pug breed has experienced some peaks and troughs in popularity during its long history. In the early 1900s numbers dwindled dramatically when the Pekingese and Pomeranian took over as the 'must have' Toy dogs.

However, thanks to the dedication of Pug enthusiasts, the breed regained ground. Modern life favors a small dog, and the Pug's distinctive looks and adaptable character mean that he suits many different lifestyles. From his distant origins in China, the Pug is now well established as a worldwide favorite.

Pictured: Black Pugs were revived by the Victorian breeder, Lady Brassey.

What should a Pug look like?

The breed has a long history, and has changed remarkably little in appearance over the centuries. So what makes a Pug look like a Pug?

Breeders of purebred dogs have a bible, known as the Breed Standard, which is a written blueprint describing what the perfect specimen should look like, what his temperament should be, and outlining the outstanding characteristics of the breed.

Of course, there is no such thing as a 'perfect' dog, but breeders aspire to produce dogs that conform as closely as possible to the picture in words presented in the Breed Standard.

In the show ring, judges use the Breed Standard as their guide, and it is the dog that, in their opinion,

comes closest to the ideal, that will win top honors.

This has significance beyond the sport of showing for it is the dogs that win in the ring that will be used for breeding. The winners of today are therefore responsible for passing on their genes to future generations and preserving the breed in its best form.

There are minor differences in the wording of the Breed Standard, depending on national Kennel Clubs, but the descriptions are broadly similar.

General appearance

The Pug is square in shape and should appear well proportioned and symmetrical. He should not be too low on the legs, but neither should he appear lean and leggy. He is refered to as 'cobby', meaning he is short in the body, well muscled and compact.

Characteristcs/temperament

The Pug combines charm and dignity. He is even-tempered with a lively, playful disposition, and a fair degree of self-confidence.

Head

The head is relatively large in proportion to the body. It is round in shape with no indentation of the skull. The muzzle is short, blunt and square; not 'upfaced', which would give the appearance of a Bulldog, nor flat-faced which would resemble a Pekingese. The nose is pushed in, but the nostrils should be large and open.

The wrinkles on the head must be well defined but not exaggerated. The nose roll – the wrinkles above the nose – should be moderate, otherwise breathing can be adversely affected.

Eyes

The Pug's large, round eyes are an outstanding feature. They are dark in color and deeply expressive; at one moment they are soft and solicitous, but they can change in a split second to being full of fire when a Pug is excited. The eyes should not protrude, and the British Standard states that there should be no white showing when a dog is looking ahead. These safeguards have been introduced to try to eliminate eye problems from the breed.

Ears

The Pug's ears are small and soft, and feel like velvet to the touch. There are two types of ear permitted in the Breed Standard: the 'rose' ear, which is a drop ear with a small fold in the middle, and a 'button' ear, where the ear flap folds forward and lies close to the skull. Button ears are favored in the show ring.

Mouth

The Pug has a wide lower jaw, and the bite (the positioning of the teeth) is slightly undershot. This means the teeth on the bottom jaw marginally overlap the teeth on the upper jaw. Neither the teeth, nor the tongue, should be visible when the mouth is closed.

Neck

The Pug carries his head proudly, and for this he needs a strong, thick neck, which is slightly arched. If the neck is too short, it would look as though the head was coming straight out of the shoulders.

Forequarters

The legs are strong, straight and positioned well under the body. They should be set well apart to give a wide chest. The shoulders must have good angulation to give the correct front movement.

Body

It is the shape of the body that gives the Pug his square appearance. He should have a rounded ribcage and a level back, so he looks strong and compact. A topline that dips at the shoulders is much frowned upon.

Hindquarters

The Pug is a strong, muscular dog for his size, and this can be seen in the powerful hindquarters. Again, the legs are set well under the body, and they should have a good bend of stifle. When viewed from behind, they should be straight and parallel; it is important that the hindquarters balance with the forequarters.

Feet

The feet should look neat; they should not have long, spread out toes, referred to as 'hare' feet, neither are they as round as 'cat' feet. Regardless of the coat color, the nails should always be black.

Tail

The Pug's tail is one of his distinguishing features. It should be set on high and curl over the hip. The tail may have a single twist, but a double twist is considered more desirable. The American Breed Standard describes a double twist as "perfection".

Movement

Viewed from the front, the forelegs should be carried well to the fore, nor turning in or out. The rear action should be strong and true. The Pug has a slight, unexaggerated roll when he is moving, which comes from the hindquarters.

Coat

The coat is fine, smooth and glossy. The fawn Pug has a double coat; a soft undercoat with a smooth, shiny outer coat. The black Pug has a fine, short, single coat.

Color

The Pug is either fawn or black.

The shades of fawn range from silver, which is a greyish fawn, to apricot, which is a warmer, golden color. It is most important that the black markings which appear on the ears, muzzle (mask), forehead and back (a trace about half an inch /1.25 cm wide which runs from then base of the skull to the tail) are well defined. The diamond or thumb-mark on the forehead is considered to be a highly desirable feature.

The black Pug should have a dark gleaming coat, with no white hairs and no hint of a brown tinge.

Size

A weight guide is given – 14-18lb (6.3-8.1kg) – which is the same for both dogs and bitches.

Summary

The written description given in the Breed Standard is precise, but it is also open to interpretation. This is the reason why breeders will produce a certain 'type', and judges will promote the dogs that fit their idea of the Breed Standard.

Fashions come and go in the dog world, and certain features may become more or less exaggerated with time. In the case of the Pug, it is vital that health issues are a top priority as problems may arise if, for example, the nose is too pushed in, the eyes are too prominent, or the nose roll is too extreme.

The Pug that has all the breed's most distinctive features – but without exaggeration – is able to live a long, happy, and healthy life.

Producing sound, healthy Pugs is the top priority for every breeder.

What do you want from your Pug?

Once you meet a Pug, your heart will be stolen. But before you take the plunge into Pug ownership, you should be absolutely certain that this is the breed to suit your family and your lifestyle.

Companionship

If you are searching for a charming little dog, full of fun, yet loving and affectionate, look no further. The Pug has been bred over many centuries to be a 'people' dog, and he excels in this role.

He wants to be with his family, joining in all the activities, or snoozing next to you on the sofa. He is the most adaptable of dogs, and will do his best to fit in with you. He will go for walks, play in the garden, travel in the car, or watch you do the housework. He is

lively and playful and, despite his doleful expression, he has a stroke of comic genius that will give you endless entertainment.

Above all, he will be your best friend, and your loyal companion.

Family dog

If you have children in the family, the Pug is a good choice, particularly if they are beyond the toddler age. This is a breed that is known for his even temper, and most will be very tolerant of children. However, it is vitally important that you are fair to your Pug and do not allow children to pester him, tease him, or make his life a misery.

A sense of mutual respect must be established where a Pug accepts the younger members of his family pack, and children understand that he is a living creature with his own special needs.

Trainability

If you want an Obedience Champion, perhaps you should be considering another breed...

There is no doubting the Pug's intelligence, but he is a thinking dog, and he will see no point in training exercises that he finds boring and repetitious.

You will need to keep one step ahead of your Pug to keep his lively mind occupied. He also needs the motivation to co-operate – in the form of tasty treats, play and praise – so pleasing you becomes his top priority.

Show dog

Do you have ambitions to exhibit your Pug in the show ring? This is a specialist sport, which often becomes highly addictive, but you do need the right dog to start with.

If you plan to show your Pug, you need to track down a show quality puppy, and train him so he will perform in the show ring, and accept the detailed 'hands on' examination that he will be subjected to when he is being judged.

You also need to accept that not every puppy with show potential develops into a top-quality specimen. The most promising puppy may not turn out as expected, so you must be prepared to love your Pug and give him a home for life, even if he doesn't make the grade.

What does your Pug want from you?

The Pug is one of the least demanding of dogs – his *raison d'etre* is to fit in with you. But although his needs are moderate, they should not be set aside. Prospective owners must make sure they can provide a loving, forever home for this exceptional little dog.

Time and commitment

Why would you take on a dog if you do not have time for him? It is a simple enough question, with a pretty straightforward answer, but all too many owners fail to find time for their family pets.

If you have a larger, more energetic breed, such as a Labrador Retriever, it is hard to ignore the fact that the dog needs exercise and training. But with a small, low-maintenance breed like the Pug, you can fall into the trap of giving him too little because he is not making demands on you.

But the reason why the Pug is such a wonderful companion dog is because he has been developed especially for this role. His job is to be with people, and if he is excluded, or ignored, he will be miserable.

No dog should be left for more than four hours a day, and with Toy breeds this is really too much. Your Pug should be taught to accept limited periods of time on his own, but he should spend the majority of every day with his people. If you cannot guarantee this, you should maybe put dog ownership on hold until your circumstances change.

Healthy lifetyle

The Pug does not require huge amounts of exercise, which is why he is suited to older owners, or those with less mobility. But if he is allowed to become a couch potato, and is fed lots of treats between meals, he will run the risk of serious health problems. It is your responsibility to keep your Pug fit and healthy throughout his life.

Mental stimulation

This is a must for all dogs, as boredom can lead to a whole range of behavioral problems. The Pug is an intelligent dog, and although he has no desire to be drilled in obedience, he needs to use his brain.

Mental stimulation can take many different forms – going on different walks so your Pug has the opportunity to discover new and exciting smells, playing games in the garden, or teaching him new tricks. It does not matter what you do; you simply need to bear in mind that a bored dog is an unhappy dog.

Extra considerations

Now you have established that the Pug is your chosen breed, you need to narrow your search so you know exactly what you are looking for.

Male or female?

With some of the larger breeds, size is an important consideration as the male is often bigger than the female. But this is not the case with Pugs as both sexes come within the same weight category.

There are some Pug owners who swear that females are more loyal and affectionate than males , and others who say the opposite – so it all comes down to personal preference.

If you opt for a female, you will need to cope with her seasonal cycle, which will start at any time from six to nine months, with seasons occurring every six to nine months thereafter. During the three-week period of a season, you will need to keep your bitch away from entire males (males that have not been neutered) to eliminate the risk of an unwanted pregnancy.

Many pet owners opt for neutering, which puts an end to the seasons, and also and has many attendant health benefits. The operation, known as spaying,

Facing page: An entire male may develop a wanderlust.

is usually carried out at some point after the first season. The best plan is to ask your vet for advice.

An entire male may not cause many problems, although some do have a stronger tendency to mark, which could include the house, unless properly trained. An entire male will also be on the lookout for bitches in season, and this may lead to difficulties, depending on your circumstances.

Neutering (castrating) a male is a relatively simple operation, and there are associated health benefits. Again, you should seek advice from your vet.

More than one?

Pugs are sociable dogs and certainly enjoy each other's company. But you would be wise to guard against the temptation of getting two puppies from the same litter, or even two of similar ages,

Unfortunately there are some unscrupulous breeders who encourage people to do this, but they are thinking purely in terms of profit, and not considering the welfare of the puppies.

Looking after one puppy is hard work, but taking on two pups at the same time is more than double the workload. House training is a nightmare as, often, you don't even know which puppy is making mistakes, and training is impossible unless you separate the two puppies and give them one-on-one attention.

The puppies will never be bored as they have each other to play with. However, the likelihood is that they will form a close bond with each other, and you will come a poor second.

If you do decide to add to your Pug population, wait at least 18 months so your first dog is fully trained and settled before taking on a puppy.

An older dog

You may decide to miss out on the puppy phase and take on an older dog instead. Such a dog may be harder to track down, but sometimes a breeder may have a youngster that is not suitable for showing, but is perfect for a family pet. In some cases, a breeder may re-home a female when her breeding career is at an end so she will enjoy the benefits of getting more individual attention.

There are advantages to taking on an older dog, as you know exactly what you are getting. But the upheaval of changing homes can be quite upsetting, so you will need to have plenty of patience during the settling in period.

Rehoming a rescued dog

Unfortunately, there are Pugs that need to be re-homed through no fault of their own. The reasons may vary from illness or death of the original owner to family breakdown, changing jobs, or even the arrival of a new baby. There are some cases where a Pug has developed behavioral problems because of poor training and socialization in his first home.

If you decide to go down this route, find out as much as you can about the Pug's history so you know exactly what you are taking on. You need to be realistic about what you are capable of achieving so you can be sure you can give the dog in question a permanent home.

Again, you need to give a rescued Pug plenty of time and patience as he settles into his new home. But if all goes well, you will have the reward of knowing that you have given your dog a second chance.

Sourcing a puppy

This is where you must be careful that your heart does not rule your head. It is so easy to look at a beautiful litter of puppies and fall for the first one you see – but has the breeder given them a good start in life? The time, care and thought that goes into planning and rearing a litter will have a huge impact on the future well-being of the puppies that are produced.

Essentially, you are looking for a fit, clean, happy, healthy puppy that is typical of the breed and is likely to live to a ripe old age. In order to avoid unnecessary heartache it is best to be patient and find the right puppy for you, from the correct source.

Finding a breeder

A good starting place is your national Kennel Club, which has a vast amount of information for both show and pet owners, easily available via the Internet. The next step would be to go to dog shows where you will be able to see a variety of Pugs. Wait until a class has been judged, and then talk to the exhibitors – particularly if you have seen a dog you particularly like the look of. Ask questions about the dog's breeding, and his temperament; this is a valuable way of gaining more information about the breed.

The exhibitors you talk to may, or may not, know about up and coming litters, but if they are unable to help, you can do some more research on the Kennel Club website. You will find contact details for breed clubs, and their secretaries are usually aware of members who have, or are expecting, litters.

There is also a list of Kennel Club registered puppies on the site, but this does not carry any guarantees beyond the fact that a litter has been registered

Opposite: You want a sound, healthy puppy that is typical of the breed.

with the Kennel Club. If the breeder is termed an 'assured breeder' (UK) or 'breeder of merit' (USA), it means that the breeder has complied with the Kennel Club guidelines for breeding a litter. Bear in mind that reputable breeders usually only breed a litter when they want a new puppy to show and, therefore, there may be a waiting list.

Buyer beware!

In your impatience to find a Pug puppy, it is all too easy to fall into the trap of going to an unsuitable source.

Avoid newspapers advertising a litter, or cards placed in shop windows. At best, these could be the result of an inexperienced pet owner breeding a litter, and although they may have done a good job, there are absolutely no guarantees – particularly regarding the choice of a sire. All too often, the

neighborhood dog will have been chosen as a good match, without any research into bloodlines and health issues.

Be especially wary of advertising on the Internet, as all may not be as it appears. There is a danger that the puppies may have come from a puppy farm, where litters of all breeds are produced purely for financial gain, with no thought for the health, temperament, or rearing of the puppies involved.

Questions, questions, questions

Telephone the breeder of the puppies and ask as many questions as you need to; a reputable breeder will be only too pleased to provide you with as much information as you require.

As well as asking about the size of the litter, the number of males and females, and the color, you should also check the health status of the parents. Like all breeds, the Pug has inherited conditions, and you need to ensure the breeder has made the necessary checks and clearances on the breeding stock that has been used.

The breeder should also be asking you questions about your family – for example, whether there is going to be someone at home during the day to look after the puppy – to make sure that your home is suitable for a Pug.

Puppy
watching

No sensible breeder should allow anyone to visit puppies when they are first born. This would be unfair on the nursing mother, who may be adapting to her new family and find strangers an intrusion. Understandably, visitors want to touch or handle puppies, which in the early stages of a puppy's life can be a little distressing for the mother and risks infection.

In the interests of all, it is best to visit puppies when they are on their feet and starting to play and run around, which is generally at five to six weeks of age.

What to look for

The puppies should be reared in the house and be living in clean and comfortable surroundings. Puppies obviously do make a mess and are not house-trained at this stage of their life, but there should be no excessive odor from them or the environment in which they are kept.

Facing page: Watch the mother interacting with her puppies.

They should have clean coats and bright eyes, with no discharge, and their rear ends should also be clean and free from any signs of matting or diarrhoea. Their nostrils should be clear and not pinched, which could cause difficulty in breathing.

The puppies should be brought up in an environment that allows them to become accustomed to all the comings and goings of a busy household. They should be used to hearing voices, the sound of the television and radio, the vacuum cleaner and washing machine, and they should be happy to be handled by different people.

This is an important part of their early education, which will prepare them for life in the outside world. If this early regime of socialization is not followed, it can result in nervous puppies that cannot cope with loud noises or with strangers, and this nervousness can stay with them forever.

When you visit the puppies they should be full of life, running around playing with each other, responding immediately to your presence. There should be no sign of nervousness or holding back – there is usually a rush to see which of the littermates reaches you first!

The mother of the puppies should be available to be seen although, depending on the age of the puppies, she may not be required to be with them constantly once they have started to eat solid food. The mother or dam, as she is known, should also be in a clean and healthy condition; she should be friendly and outgoing, ready to greet you and show off her puppies.

It is unlikely that you will see the puppies' father, as in most cases a breeder will travel to use a stud dog that complements the bitch and her bloodlines. However, the breeder should have photos available, and details of his show record.

Picking a show puppy

If you are aiming to find a puppy with show potential, it is a good idea to take an experienced person with you who understands the finer points of the Breed Standard.

The best age to choose a puppy is between 8 and 10 weeks, when the pups have developed sufficiently to assess conformation, movement and personality.

A Pug puppy with show potential should have a friendly, outgoing temperament, and, ideally, a sense of self-importance, indicating he is happy to show off before a crowd. He should have the basic, square Pug shape and be heavier than expected when picked up, epitomizing the Breed Standard requirement to be *multum in parvo*.

He should have a well-shaped head with a broad underjaw, and the promise of some wrinkle on his head. The eyes should be dark and expressive; the front legs should be straight with space between for a broad chest. The topline should be level, and the tail should already be carried over the back and beginning to curl. Both black and fawn-colored Pugs should have jet-black pigmentation, and this includes black nails on fawn dogs.

Even if you find a puppy that answers all these credentials, there is no certainty that he will make the grade as a show dog. Dogs can change as they develop – for better and for worse – so there is always an element of luck involved.

Facing page: A Pug may go through different phases as he grows and matures.

A Pug-friendly home

It will soon be time to bring your Pug puppy home, but before you do this, there is much to plan in advance and consider. While the whole process of introducing a puppy to his new home is very exciting for the family, it will possibly be very daunting for the puppy.

House rules

First of all, decide all the ground rules before the puppy comes into your home, and make sure that the whole family sticks to them. A puppy needs consistent handling by everyone or he will very quickly become confused.

The rules you establish are very much a matter of personal preference; if you are happy to allow your Pug on the sofa that is fine. But, remember, once you set a precedent, it is very difficult to change it. So if your

Pug returns from a muddy walk and jumps on the sofa you only have yourself to blame!

Safety in the home

You will need to check your home to ensure that your puppy will be safe. A Pug puppy is naturally curious and will investigate everything he comes across with his mouth. This is potentially very hazardous, so you need to go round the house and assess it from a puppy's perspective.

Electric cables need to be secured out of reach, breakable ornaments and houseplants need to be removed (many plants are toxic to dogs), and if you have children, toys need to be tidied away. This also applies to small items of clothing, such as tights, which can be chewed and swallowed, causing major problems. Cleaning materials and detergents can pose a danger, so these should be shut away in cupboards.

In the garden

The garden must be securely fenced, and gates should be checked to ensure they have secure fastenings. Obviously a Pug is not going to leap over high fences, but all boundaries should be checked for possible escape routes.

If you are a keen gardener, you may decide to

allocate an area of the garden for your puppy and fence off your prize plants. You will also need to decide on a toileting area, as this will help the process of house-training (see page 100), and will make cleaning up easier.

If you have a pond, make sure the puppy cannot access it, and you should also check plants that are poisonous to dogs. Lists can be found on the Internet (see Useful addresses).

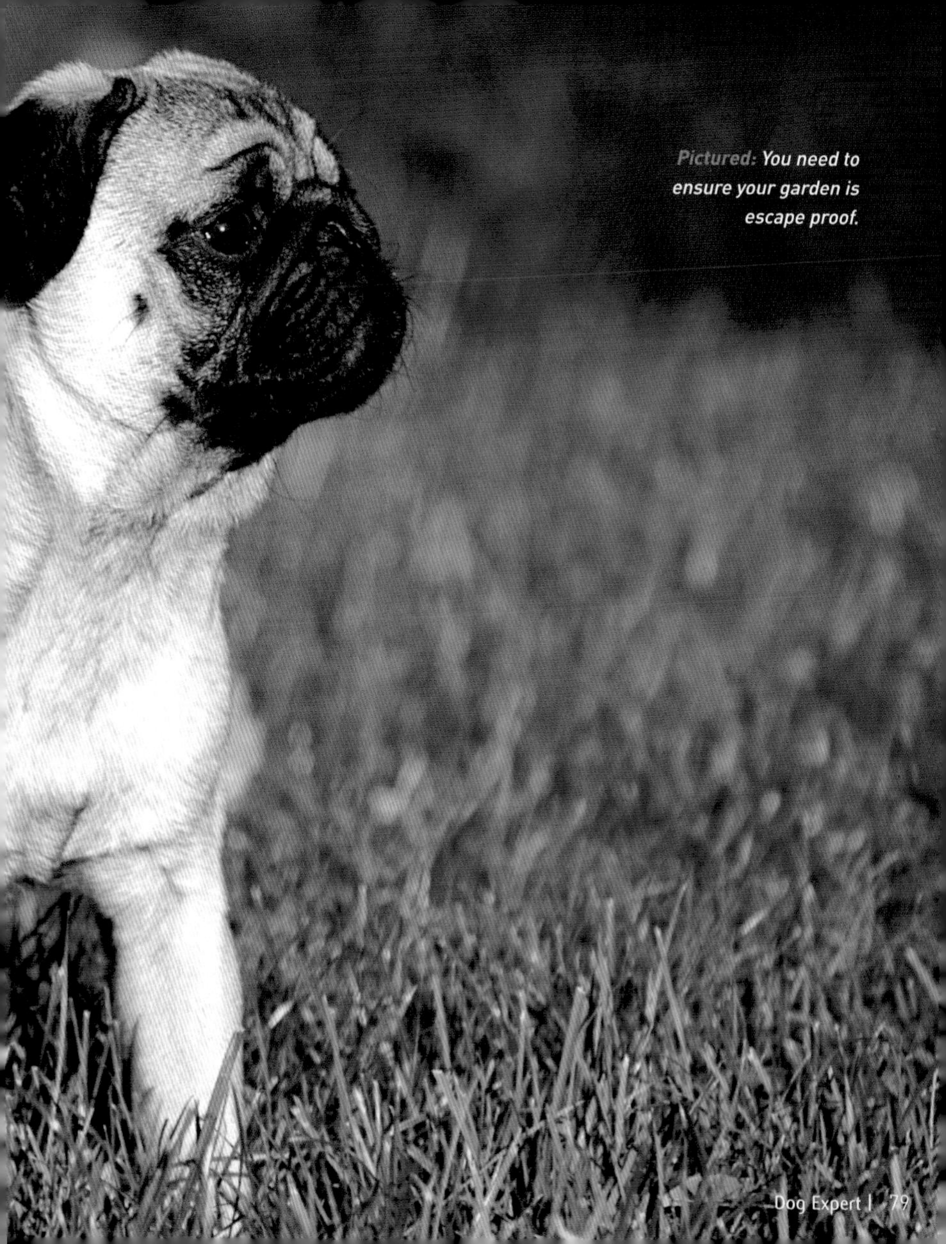

Pictured: You need to ensure your garden is escape proof.

Finding a vet

It is a good idea to register with a vet before you collect your puppy. When considering which vet to choose, you can consult friends who own dogs. Breed clubs can also provide lists of recommended vets, including, in some cases, veterinarians with special knowledge of Pugs.

Schedule an appointment with the vet you are considering. Discuss your dog and his specific needs, and from this meeting you will be able to see if you feel comfortable with what is being offered. It will also give you an opportunity to take a look at the facility. Make sure it looks and smells clean. Check what range of services it provides and ask how emergency after-hours calls are handled.

Buying equipment

Shopping is the fun part of preparing for your new puppy. You will almost certainly make additions as you go along, but there are some essential items of equipment you will need from the start.

Indoor crate

This is an invaluable investment, providing your puppy with his own personal space – and you with peace of mind. Make sure you buy a crate that is big

Facing page: Your Pug will be safe and secure if he travels in a crate.

enough for your Pug to use when he is fully grown. Many adult dogs choose their crate if the door is left open, rather than a dog bed.

The best place to locate a crate is in the kitchen or in a next-door utility room. Your puppy does not want to be cut off from his new family, but he needs somewhere he can rest undisturbed. The place you choose should be warm in the winter, cool in the summer, and free from drafts. Avoid using a conservatory, as these are subject to extremes of temperature, which is highly unsuitable for a dog of any age.

When introducing a crate, you want the puppy to associate it with being a safe and happy place to return to and sleep in. Never use the crate as a place of punishment. It should be used when your puppy needs to rest, at times when you cannot supervise him, and to keep him safe overnight. It can also be useful when you are traveling, staying away in a hotel, or as a safe place to put your youngster if you have a visitor who has an allergy to, or simply does not like, dogs!

Dog beds

There is an amazing array of dog beds on the market
– from four-posters to igloos, wicker baskets,
beanbags and duvets, there is something to suit
every taste, and every pocket. However, you would
be advised to wait until your puppy is beyond the
chewing phase before making a major investment.
On purely practical grounds, a plastic bed, lined
with soft bedding, is comfortable, easy to clean and
virtually indestructible.

Bedding

The best type of bedding is synthetic fleece, which you can buy in a variety of sizes. This is warm and cozy, with the added advantage that it allows moisture to soak through, which is useful when you are house-training. A small puppy cannot last the whole night without relieving himself, and this type of bedding ensures he still has a dry bed.

Synthetic bedding is machine washable and easy to dry. Buy at least two pieces so you always have one to use while the other is in the wash.

Bowls

As a short-nosed breed, the Pug prefers a feeding bowl that is not too deep, as this makes it easier to reach his food.

Again, there are many different bowls to choose from, but those made of stainless steel are the most hard-wearing and hygienic. You will also need to provide a bowl for fresh drinking water. This should be relatively shallow, and it helps if it has a rubber base so it does not slide across the floor.

Collar and leash

To start with, all you need is a lightweight nylon collar and leash. A puppy will quickly outgrow his first collar, so the next stage is to buy an adjustable collar, which you can use until your Pug is fully grown. You can then be tempted by the dazzling displays of collars and leashes, which come in a huge range of designs, colors and materials.

Bear in mind that a wide collar is not comfortable for a Pug, and the leash must have a secure trigger fastening. If you opt for a harness, make sure it is fitted by an expert, so that your Pug is safe, secure and comfortable.

Below: When your Pug is fully grown you can choose from the vast array of collars that are on offer.

ID

Your Pug must have some form of identity when he goes out in public places. Ideally, he should have an engraved disc attached to his collar with your contact details, and he should also a permanent form of ID, such as a tattoo or a microchip.

Grooming equipment

The Pug's coat is easy to care for, but there are a few essential items which include:

- Cotton (cotton-wool) pads to wipe around the eyes and face

- A soft brush for puppy grooming

- A stiff-bristled brush for adult grooming

- A fine-toothed comb (this is to remove the undercoat on fawn Pugs when they are shedding)

- Guillotine nail clippers

- Toothbrush and toothpaste.

For more information on grooming, see page 112.

Toys

The Pug is playful as a puppy, and many adults will continue to enjoy toys throughout their lives. Soft toys are most certainly a favorite, but you need to be careful during the puppy phase as they can easily be destroyed. You will also find that your Pug puppy is quite happy to play with inexpensive, homemade items such as the cardboard center of a toilet roll, or old woollen socks made safely into a ball.

Boredom busting toys, such as Kongs, which can be filled with food, provide useful occupation at times when you have to leave your Pug on his own.

Facing page: Provide a variety of toys or your puppy will find his own fun!

Settling in

The big day has finally come and it is time to collect your puppy. Check with the breeder to see if you can arrive in the morning. This will allow your puppy more time to settle once he is home. If possible, ask for a piece of bedding that has been in with the litter. This will have a familiar smell, and will help your puppy to make the transition to his new home.

Once your puppy arrives, try to keep the environment as quiet as possible. Avoid having too many people crowding him – your friends can always come and meet your new Pug another day, once he is settled in.

Let your puppy explore the garden, and if he relieves himself, give him lots of praise – you may as well start as you mean to go on! Next, take your puppy into the kitchen/utility room and show him his sleeping quarters. You can start introducing him to his crate by throwing in a treat, and praising him when he goes inside. You can follow this up by feeding your puppy in his crate as this will help to build up a good association.

Although tempting, try not to lavish too much attention on your puppy too quickly; this is a scary situation for him and he needs time to get used to both the environment and his new family.

Meeting the family

If you have children in the family, you need to keep everything as calm as possible. The arrival of a new puppy is hugely exciting for them, but it may be worrying for the pup if he is not used to children.

The best plan is to get the children to sit on the floor and give each of them a treat. Each child can then call the puppy, stroke him, and offer a treat. In this way the puppy is standing on his own four feet and making the decisions rather than being forced into interactions he may find stressful.

It is a good idea to impose a rule, right from the start, that the children are not allowed to pick up or carry the puppy. They can cuddle him when they are sitting on the floor. This may sound a little severe, but a wriggly puppy can be dropped in an instant, sometimes with disastrous consequences

Involve all family members with the day-to-day care of your puppy; this will enable the bond to develop with the whole family as opposed to just one person. Encourage the children to train and reward the puppy, teaching him to follow their commands without question.

The animal family

If you already have a dog, you need to introduce your puppy tactfully so relations get off on a good footing.

Your adult dog may be allowed to meet the puppy at the breeder's home which is ideal as the older dog will not feel threatened if he is away from his own home. But if this is not possible, allow your dog to smell the puppy's bedding (the bedding supplied by the breeder is fine) before they actually meet so he familiarizes himself with the puppy's scent.

Pictured: *A puppy and a cat can become the best of friends.*

The garden is the best place for introducing the puppy, as the adult will regard it as neutral territory. He will probably take a great interest in the puppy and sniff him all over. Most puppies are naturally submissive in this situation, and your pup may lick the other dog's mouth or roll over on to his back.

You will only need to intervene if the older dog is too boisterous, and alarms the puppy. In this case, it is a good idea to put the adult on a lead so you have some measure of control.

It rarely takes long for an adult to accept a puppy, particularly if you make a big fuss of the older dog so that he still feels special. However, do not take any risks and supervise all interactions for the first few weeks. If you do need to leave the dogs alone, always make sure your puppy is safe in his crate.

Meeting a cat should be supervised in a similar way, but do not allow your puppy to be rough. Most cats are more than capable of looking after themselves, but care must be taken at the first meeting to prevent any unwanted animosity, as this will only progress as the puppy grows.

The Pug does not have a strong prey drive so he should not be preoccupied with chasing the cat, but if your puppy tries do this, put a stop to it immediately. Generally, the Pug-feline relationship should not cause many problems. Indeed, many Pugs and cats become the best of friends.

Feeding

The breeder will generally provide enough food for the first few days so the puppy does not have to cope with a change in diet – and possible digestive upset – along with all the stress of moving home.

Some puppies eat all their food from the first meal onwards, others are more concerned by their new surroundings and are too distracted to eat. Do not worry unduly if your puppy seems disinterested in his food for the first day or so. Give him 10 minutes to eat what he wants and then remove the leftovers and start afresh at the next meal.

Do not make the mistake of trying to tempt his appetite with tasty treats or you will end up with a faddy feeder.

Obviously if you have any concerns about your puppy in the first few days, seek advice from your vet.

The first night

Your puppy will have spent the first weeks of his life constantly with his mother or curled up with his siblings. He is then taken from everything he knows as familiar, often lavished with attention by his new family for several hours, and then comes bed time. It is at this time that he is placed in his crate, all the lights are switched off, and he is abandoned – at least that is how he feels.

The best plan is to establish a night-time routine, and then stick to it so that your puppy knows what is expected of him. Take your puppy out into the garden to relieve himself, and then settle him in his crate.

Some people leave a low light on for the puppy at night for the first week, considering that he may like to become accustomed to his new home before being left entirely in the dark. Others have tried a radio as company or a ticking clock.

Like people, puppies are all individuals and what works for one, does not necessarily work for another, so it is a matter of trial and error.

Be very positive when you leave your puppy on his own. Do not linger, or keep returning; this will make the situation more difficult. It is inevitable that he will protest to begin with, but if you stick to your routine, he will accept that he gets left at night – but you always return in the morning.

Facing page: It is inevitable that your puppy will feel lonely for the first few nights.

Rescued dogs

Settling an older, rescued dog in the home is very similar to a puppy in as much as you will need to make the same preparations regarding his homecoming. As with a puppy, an older dog will need you to be consistent, so start as you mean to go on.

There is often an initial honeymoon period when you bring a rescued dog home, where he will be on his best behavior for the first few weeks. It is after these first couple of weeks that the true nature of the dog will show, so be prepared for subtle changes in his behavior. It may be advisable to register with a training club, so you can seek advice on any training or behavioral issues at an early stage.

Above all, remember that a rescued dog ceases to be a rescued dog the moment he enters his forever home. He is now part of the family.

Facing page: It can be very rewarding to give a Pug a second chance.

House training

This is easier than you think and your puppy will usually get the idea of what is required within the first few days.

When you were preparing for your puppy's homecoming, you will have allocated a toileting area in your garden. You need to take your puppy to this area every time he needs to relieve himself so he builds up an association and knows why you have brought him out to the garden.

Establish a routine and make sure you take your puppy out at the following times:

- First thing in the morning

- After mealtimes

- On waking from a sleep
  Following a play session

- Last thing at night.

A puppy should be taken out to relieve himself every two hours as an absolute minimum. If you can manage an hourly trip, so much the better. The more your puppy gets it 'right', the quicker he will learn to be clean in the house.

It helps if you use a verbal cue, such as "Busy", when your pup is performing and, in time, this will trigger the desired response.

Do not be tempted to put your puppy out on the

doorstep in the hope that he will toilet on his own. Most pups simply sit there, waiting to get back inside the house! No matter how bad the weather is, accompany your puppy and give him lots of praise when he performs correctly.

Do not rush back inside as soon as he has finished. Your puppy might start to delay in the hope of prolonging his time outside with you. Praise him, have a quick game – and then you can both return indoors.

When accidents happen

No matter how vigilant you are, there are bound to be accidents. If you witness the accident, take your puppy outside immediately, and give him lots of praise if he finishes his business out there.

If you are not there when he has an accident, do not scold him when you discover what has happened. He will not remember what he has done and will not understand why you are cross with him. Simply clean it up and resolve to be more vigilant next time.

Make sure you use a deodorizer, available in pet stores, when you clean up, otherwise your pup will be drawn to the smell and may be tempted to use the same spot again.

Choosing
a diet

There are so many different types of dog food to choose from, it can be bewildering for the first-time owner. The priority is to find a good-quality, well-balanced diet that is suited to your Pug's individual needs.

When choosing a diet, there are basically three categories to choose from:

Complete

This is probably the most popular diet as it is easy to feed and is specially formulated with all the nutrients your dog needs. This means that you should not add any supplements or you may upset the nutritional balance.

Most complete diets come in different life stages: puppy, adult maintenance and senior. This means that your Pug is getting what he needs as he is

growing, during his adulthood, and then when he becomes older.

There are many different brands to choose from so it is advisable to seek advice from your puppy's breeder, who will have lengthy experience of feeding Pugs.

Canned/pouches

This type of food is usually fed with hard biscuit, and most Pugs find it very appetizing. However, the ingredients – and the nutritional value – do vary significantly between the different brands so you will need to check the label.

Homemade and natural diets

There are some owners who like to prepare meals especially for their dogs – and it is probably much appreciated. The danger is that although the food is tasty, and your Pug may appreciate the variety, you cannot be sure that it has the correct nutritional balance.

If this is a route you want to go down, you will need to find out the exact ratio of fats, carbohydrates, proteins, minerals and vitamins that are needed, which is quite an undertaking.

Some owners advocate feeding a diet as close as possible to what would be available if dogs were

living wild, such as raw, meaty bones. This is sometimes referred to as the BARF (Bones And Raw Food or Biologically Appropriate Raw Food) diet. There is plenty of information about this method of feeding available on the internet or in books.

Feeding regime

When your puppy arrives in his new home he will need four meals, evenly spaced throughout the day. You may decide to keep to the diet recommended by your puppy's breeder, and if your pup is thriving there is no need to change. However, if your puppy is not doing well on the food, or you have problems with supply, you will need to make a change.

When switching diets, it is very important to do it on a gradual basis, changing over from one food to the next a little at a time, and spreading the transition over a week to 10 days. This will avoid the risk of digestive upset.

When your puppy is around 12 weeks, you can cut out one of his meals; he may well have started to leave some of his food, indicating he is ready to do this. By six months, he can move on to two meals a day – a regime that will suit him for the rest of his life.

Bones and chews

Puppies love to chew, and many adults also enjoy gnawing on a bone. However, they must be hard and uncooked. Rib bones and poultry bones should always be avoided as they can splinter and cause major problems. Dental chews, and some of the manufactured rawhide chews, are safe, but they should only be given under supervision.

Another safe option is to give your Pug a hard, dog biscuit, which he will break up into smaller pieces and will, therefore, be easily consumed.

Ideal weight

In order to help to keep your Pug in good health it is necessary to monitor his weight. It is all too easy for the pounds to pile on, and this can result in serious health problems.

With a Pug, it is easy to see if he is gaining weight as he has a close-fitting coat. But even so, you can sometimes fail to see what is happening over a period of time – particularly if your Pug looks at you with his large doleful eyes, and tells you how hungry he is!

In order to keep a close check on his weight, get into the habit of visiting your veterinary surgery on a monthly basis so that you can weigh him. You can keep a record of his weight, and then you are able to make the necessary adjustments.

If you are concerned that your Pug is putting on too much weight, consult your vet who will help you to plan a suitable diet.

Pictured: You need to keep a close check on your Pug's weight.

Caring for your pug

The Pug is a relatively easy breed to care for, but like all animals he has his own special needs, which you must take on board.

Grooming

The Pug has a short, close-fitting coat that requires minimal grooming. Both black and fawn pugs have a smooth, fine coat; black Pugs have a single coat, fawn Pugs have a topcoat and a soft undercoat. This does not make much difference when it comes to grooming, although seasonal shedding will be more obvious in fawn-colored dogs.

A Pug's coat does not get knotted and tangled, but it should still be groomed on a weekly basis. This allows you to keep a close check on your Pug's overall condition as well as keeping his coat in good order. Remember, brushing the coat is good for the circulation.

Use a soft brush for a puppy so that he gets used to the procedure. When your Pug is fully grown you can change over to a stiff bristle brush, which is ideal for removing dirt and debris. When your Pug is shedding, a pin brush or a fine-toothed comb will help to remove the dead hair.

Nose roll

This is the area just above the nose where there is a deep fold of the skin. Nose rolls should not be too exaggerated, but some are more pronounced than others and will, therefore, need more attention.

Regardless of the size of nose roll, you should get into the habit of checking it on a daily basis. If the skin becomes moist and dirty, it can become infected. This can be treated by the vet, but it will be very sore and uncomfortable for your Pug.

All you need to do is wipe the nose roll clean, using cotton (cotton-wool) or a cotton bud and then apply some olive oil, which prevents the skin from becoming too dry. Do not use Vaseline as this tends to clog the nose roll and prevents the air getting to it.

Eyes

Check the eyes for signs of soreness or discharge. You can use a piece of cotton (cotton-wool) – a separate piece for each eye – and wipe away any debris.

Start off with a bristle brush.

A pin brush helps to remove the dead hair.

The nose roll should be cleaned daily.

Wipe the eyes so they are free from debris.

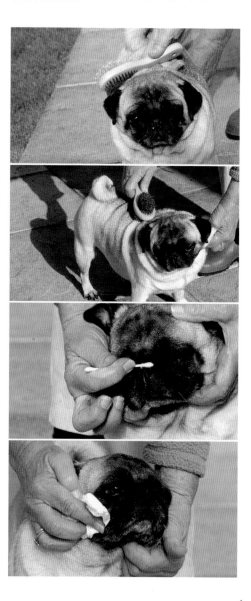

Ears

The ears should be clean and free from odor. You can buy specially manufactured ear wipes, or you can use a piece of cotton to clean them if necessary. Do not probe into the ear canal or you risk doing more harm than good.

Teeth

Dental disease is becoming more prevalent among dogs so teeth cleaning should be seen as an essential part of your care regime. The build-up of tartar on the teeth can result in tooth decay, gum infection and bad breath, and if it is allowed to accumulate, it may need to be removed under anesthetic.

When your Pug is still a puppy accustom him to teeth cleaning so it becomes a matter of routine. Dog toothpaste comes in a variety of meaty flavours, which your Pug will like, so you can start by putting some toothpaste on your finger and gently rubbing his teeth. You can then progress to using a finger brush or a toothbrush, whichever you find most convenient. Remember to reward your Pug when he co-operates.

Nails

Nail trimming is a task dreaded by many owners – and many dogs – but, again, if you start early on, your Pug will get used to the procedure. Pugs are

Clean the ears but do not probe into the ear canal.

Accustom your Pug to teeth cleaning from an early age.

Take care when trimming the nails.

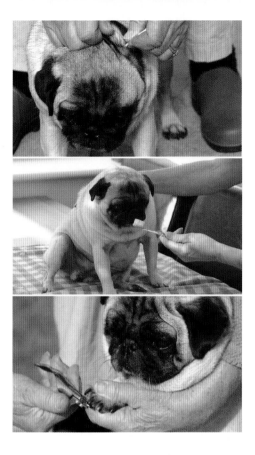

bred to have dark nails, and these are harder to trim than white nails as you cannot see the quick (the vein that runs through the nail), which will bleed if it is nicked. The best policy is to trim little and often so the nails don't grow too long, and you do not risk cutting too much and catching the quick.

If you are worried about trimming your Pug's nails, go to your vet so you can see it done properly. If you are still concerned, you can always use the services of a professional groomer.

Exercise

The Pug is very adaptable when it comes to exercise, but this does not mean that he is content with the bare minimum.

Exercise gives a dog the opportunity to use his nose and investigate new sights and smells, so even if he does not go for miles, he will appreciate varied walks. If you are a keen walker, the sturdy little Pug will be an excellent companion and will keep going for as long as you do.

If, for any reason, your time is limited, it is useful if you can teach your Pug to retrieve a toy. He will expend a lot of energy playing this game and he will also enjoy the mental stimulation.

The older Pug

We are fortunate the Pug has a good life expectancy, and you will not notice any significant changes in your Pug until he reaches double figures. Obviously all Pugs are individuals and some will show signs of ageing earlier than others.

The older Pug will sleep more, and he may be reluctant to go for longer walks. You may also see signs of stiffness when he gets up from his bed. Some older Pugs may have impaired vision, and some may become a little deaf.

If you treat your older Pug with kindness and consideration, he will enjoy his later years and suffer the minimum of discomfort. It is advisable to switch him over to a senior diet, which is more suited to his needs, and you may need to adjust the quantity, as he will not be burning up the calories as he did when he was younger and more energetic. Make sure his sleeping quarters are warm and free from drafts, and, if he gets wet, make sure you dry him thoroughly.

Most important of all, be guided by your Pug. He will have good days when he feels up to a longer walk, and days when he would prefer to potter in the garden. If you have a younger dog at home this may well stimulate your Pug, but make sure he is not pestered as he needs to rest undisturbed when he is tired.

Letting go

Inevitably there comes a time when your Pug is not enjoying a good quality of life, and you need to make the painful decision to let him go. We would all wish that our dogs died painlessly in their sleep, but this is rarely the case.

However, we can allow our dogs to die with dignity, and to suffer as a little as possible, and this should be our way of saying thank you for the wonderful companionship they have given us.

When you feel the time is drawing close, talk to your vet who will be able to make an objective assessment of your Pug's condition and will help you to make the right decision.

This is the hardest thing you will ever have to do as a dog owner, and it is only natural to grieve for your beloved Pug. But eventually, you will be able to look back on the happy memories of times spent together, and this will bring much comfort. You may, in time, feel that your life is not complete without a Pug, and you feel ready to welcome a new puppy into your home.

Social skills

To live in the modern world, without fears and anxieties, a Pug needs to receive an education in social skills so that he learns to cope with a wide variety of situations.

Early learning

The breeder will have started a program of
socialization, getting the puppies used to all
the sights and sounds of a busy household. You
need to continue this when your pup arrives in
his new home, making sure he is not worried by
household equipment, such as the vacuum cleaner
or the washing machine, and that he gets used to
unexpected noises from the radio and television.

It is important that you handle your puppy on a
regular basis so he will accept grooming and other
routine care, and will not be worried if he has to be
examined by the vet.

To begin with, your puppy needs to get used to all the
members of his new family, but then you should give
him the opportunity to meet friends and other people
who come to the house. A Pug puppy is naturally
friendly and out-going, so this should not cause any
problems, particularly if his new friends are well
supplied with treats!

Make sure your puppy has the chance to meet and
play with children, even if you don't have any yourself,
so he learns that people come in small sizes, too.

The outside world

When your puppy has completed his vaccinations, he is ready to venture into the outside world. Most Pugs are reasonably bold, but for a small puppy there is a lot to take on board, so do not swamp him with too many new experiences when you first set out.

The best plan is to start in a quiet area with light traffic, and only progress to a busier place when your puppy is ready. There is so much to see and hear – people (perhaps carrying bags or umbrellas), pushchairs, bicycles, cars, lorries, machinery – so give your puppy a chance to take it all in.

Pictured: Progress at a speed that your Pug is comfortable with.

If he does appear worried, do not fall into the trap of sympathizing with him, or worse still, picking him up. This will only teach your pup that he had a good reason to be worried and, with luck, you will 'rescue' him if he feels scared.

Instead, give a little space so he does not have to confront whatever he is frightened of, and distract him with a few treats. Then encourage him to walk past, using a calm, no-nonsense approach. Your pup will take the lead from you, and will realize there is nothing to fear.

Your pup also needs to continue his education in canine manners, started by his mother and by his littermates, as he needs to be able to greet all dogs calmly and confidently. If you have a friend who has a dog of sound temperament, this is an ideal beginning. As your puppy gets older and more established, you can widen his circle of canine acquaintances.

Pictured: A well-socialized Pug has a calm and confident outlook on life.

Training classes

A training class will give your Pug the opportunity to interact with other dogs, and he will also learn to focus on you in a different, distracting environment.

Before you go along with your puppy, it is worth attending a class as an observer to make sure you are happy with what goes on.

Find out the following:

- How much training experience do the instructors have?

- Are the classes divided into appropriate age categories?

- Do the instructors have experience training Toy dogs and Pugs in particular?

- Do they use positive, reward-based training methods?

If the training class is well run, it is certainly worth attending. Both you and your Pug will learn useful training exercises, it will increase his social skills, and you will have the chance to talk to lots of like-minded dog enthusiasts.

Pictured: A Pug needs to learn how to relate to other dogs.

Training guidelines

The Pug is a bright little dog and he is easy to teach, as long as you make his training sessions enjoyable. You will be keen to get started, but in your rush to get his training underway, do not neglect the fundamentals which could mean the difference between success and failure.

When you start training, try to observe the following guidelines:

- Choose an area that is free from distractions so your puppy will focus on you. You can move on to a more challenging environment as your pup progresses.

- Do not train your puppy just after he has eaten or when you have returned from exercise. He will either be too full, or too tired, to concentrate.

- Do not train if you are in a bad mood, or if you are short of time – these sessions always end in disaster!

- Make sure you have a reward your Pup values – tasty treats, such as cheese or cooked liver, or an extra special toy.

- If you are using treats, make sure they are bite-sized, otherwise you will lose momentum when your pup stops to chew on his treat.

- Keep your verbal cues simple, and always use the same one for each exercise. For example, when you ask your puppy to go into the Down position, the cue is "Down", not "Lie Down", Get Down", or anything else... Remember, your Pug does not speak English; he associates the sound of the word with the action.

- If your Pug is finding an exercise difficult, break it down into small steps so it is easier to understand.

- Do not train for too long, particularly with a young puppy, who has a very short attention span, and always end training sessions on a positive note.

- Do not make your training sessions boring and repetitious; your Pug will simply switch off.

- Above all, have fun, so you and your Pug both enjoy spending quality time together.

First lessons

A Pug puppy will soak up new experiences like a sponge, so training should start from the time your pup arrives in his new home. It is so much easier to teach good habits rather than trying to correct your puppy when he has established an undesirable pattern of behavior.

Wearing a collar

- Some puppies think nothing of wearing a collar, while others act as if they are being strangled! It is best to accustom your pup to wearing a soft collar for a few minutes at a time until he gets used to it.

- Fit the collar so that you can get at least two fingers between the collar and his neck. Then have a game to distract his attention. This will work for a few moments; then he will stop, put his back leg up behind his neck and scratch away at the peculiar itchy thing round his neck, which feels so odd.

- Bend down, rotate the collar, pat him on the head and distract him by playing with a toy or giving him a treat. Once he has worn the collar for a few minutes each day, he will soon ignore it and become used to it.

- Remember, never leave the collar on the puppy unsupervised, especially when he is outside in the garden.

Walking on the lead

- Once your puppy is used to the collar, take him outside into your secure garden where there are no distractions.

- Attach the leash and, to begin with, allow him to wander with the leash trailing, making sure it does not become snagged up. Then pick up the leash and follow the pup where he wants to go; he needs to get used to the sensation of being attached to you.

- The next stage is to get your Pug to follow you, and for this you will need some tasty treats. You can show him a treat in your hand, and then encourage him to follow you. Walk a few paces, and if he is co-operating, stop and reward him. If he puts on the brakes, simply change direction and lure him with the treat.

- When your puppy is walking confidently alongside you, introduce a verbal cue "Heel" if your puppy is in the correct position. You can then graduate to walking your puppy outside the home – as long as he has completed his vaccination program – starting in quiet areas and building up to busier environments.

- Do not expect too much of your puppy too soon when you are leash walking away from home. He will be distracted by all the new sights and sounds, so concentrating on lead training will be difficult for him. Give him a chance to look and see, and reward him frequently when he is walking forward confidently on a loose leash.

Come when called

Teaching a reliable recall is invaluable for both you and your Pug. You are secure in the knowledge that he will come back when he is called, and your Pug benefits from being allowed off the leash when he has the freedom to investigate all the exciting new scents he comes across.

A Pug likes to be with his people and so he is unlikely to stray too far away. However, he may pick up an interesting scent or become distracted by meeting another dog. Obviously, you can allow him a little leeway, but you do want a dog that will come when he is called.

- The breeder may have started this lesson, simply by calling the puppies to "Come" when it is dinnertime, or when they are moving from one place to another.

- You can build on this when your puppy arrives in his new home, calling him to "Come" when he is in a confined space, such as the kitchen. This is a good place to build up a positive association with the verbal cue – particularly if you ask your puppy to "Come" to get his dinner!

- The next stage is to transfer the lesson to the garden. Arm yourself with some treats, and wait until your puppy is distracted. Then call him, using a higher-pitched, excited tone of voice. At this stage, a puppy wants to be with you, so capitalize on this and keep practicing the verbal cue, and rewarding your puppy with a treat and lots of praise when he comes to you.

- Now you are ready to introduce some distractions. Try calling him when someone else is in the garden, or wait a few minutes until he is investigating a really interesting scent. When he responds, make a really big fuss of him and give him some extra treats so he knows it is worth his while to come to you. If your puppy responds, immediately reward him with a treat.

- If he is slow to come, run away a few steps and then call again, making yourself sound really exciting. Jump up and down, open your arms wide to welcome him; it doesn't matter how silly you look, he needs to see you as the most fun person in the world.

- When you have a reliable recall in the garden, you can venture into the outside world. Do not be too ambitious to begin with; try a recall in a quiet place with the minimum of distractions and only progress to more challenging environments if your Pug is responding well.

- Do not make the mistake of only asking your dog to come at the end of a walk. What is the incentive in coming back to you if all you do is clip on his leash and head for home? Instead, call your dog at random times throughout the walk, giving him a treat and a stroke, and then letting him go free again. In this way, coming to you is always rewarding, and does not signal the end of his free run.

Pictured: Make sure that coming back to you is always a rewarding experience.

Stationary exercises

The Sit and Down are easy to teach, and mastering these exercises will be rewarding for both you and your Pug.

Sit

The best method is to lure your Pug into position, and for this you can use a treat, a toy, or his food bowl.

- Hold the reward (a treat or food bowl) above his head. As he looks up, he will lower his hindquarters and go into a sit.

- Practice this a few times and when your puppy understands what you are asking, introduce the verbal cue "Sit".

- When your Pug understands the exercise, he will respond to the verbal cue alone, and you will not need to reward him every time he sits. However, it is a good idea to give him a treat on a random basis when he co-operates to keep him guessing!

Down

This is an important lesson, and can be a lifesaver if an emergency arises and you need to bring your Pug to an instant halt.

- You can start with your dog in a Sit or a Stand for this exercise. Stand or kneel in front of him and show him you have a treat in your hand.

- Hold the treat just in front of his nose and slowly lower it towards the ground, between his front legs.

- As your Pug follows the treat he will go down on his front legs and, in a few moments, his hindquarters will follow.

- Close your hand over the treat so he doesn't cheat and get the treat before he is in the correct position. As soon as he is in the Down, give him the treat and lots of praise.

- Keep practicing, and when your Pug understands what you want, introduce the verbal cue "Down".

Control
exercises

These exercises are not the most exciting, but they are useful in a variety of situations. They also teach your Pug that you are someone to be respected, and if he co-operates, he is always rewarded for making the right decision.

Wait

This exercise teaches your Pug to "Wait" in position until you give the next command; it differs from the Stay exercise where he must stay where you have left him for a more prolonged period. The most useful application of "Wait" is when you are getting your dog out of the car and you need him to stay in position until you clip on his leash.

- Start with your puppy on the leash to give you a greater chance of success. Ask him to "Sit" and stand in front him. Step back one pace, holding your hand, palm flat, facing him. Wait a second

and then come back to stand in front of him. You can then reward him and release him with a word, such as "okay".

- Practice this a few times, waiting a little longer before you reward him, and then introduce the verbal cue "Wait".

- You can reinforce the lesson by using it in different situations, such as asking your Pug to "Wait" before you put his food bowl down.

Stay

You need to differentiate this exercise from the Wait by using a different hand signal and a different verbal cue.

- Start with your Pug in the Down as he most likely to be secure in this position. Stand by his side and then step forwards, with your hand held back, palm facing the dog.

- Step back, release him, and then reward him. Practice until your Pug understands the exercise and then introduce the verbal cue "Stay".

- Gradually increase the distance you can leave your puppy, and increase the challenge by walking around him – and even stepping over him – so that he learns he must "Stay" until you release him.

Leave

A response to this verbal cue means that your Pug will learn to give up a toy on request, and it follows that he will give up anything when he is asked, which is very useful if he has got hold of a forbidden object. You can also use it if you catch him red-handed raiding the bin, or digging up a prized plant in the garden.

Some Pugs can be a little possessive over their toys, and so this lesson should be taught from an early age.

- The "Leave" command can be taught quite easily when you are first playing with your puppy. As you gently take a toy from his mouth, introduce the verbal cue, "Leave", and then praise him.

- If he is reluctant, swap the toy for another toy or a treat. This will usually do the trick.

- Do not try to pull the toy from his mouth if he refuses to give it up, as this will only make him keener to hang on to it. Let the toy go 'dead' in your hand, and then swap it for a new, exciting toy, so this becomes the better option.

- Remember to make a big fuss of your Pug when he co-operates. If he is rewarded with verbal praise, plus a game with a toy or a tasty treat, he will learn that "leave" means that he will get something even better.

Facing page: If your Pug gives up something he values on request, make sure he is rewarded.

Opportunities for Pugs

The Pug is an intelligent dog and enjoys the chance to use his brain. In order to bring out his full character and potential, you may decide to get involved with some of the canine sports and activities on offer.

Good Citizen Scheme

The Kennel Club Good Citizen Scheme was introduced to promote responsible dog ownership, and to teach dogs basic good manners. In the US there is one test; in the UK there are four award levels: Puppy Foundation, Bronze, Silver and Gold.

Exercises within the scheme include:

- Walking on lead

- Road walking

- Control at door/gate.

- Food manners

- Recall

- Stay

- Send to bed

- Emergency stop.

Competitive obedience

The Pug is not a natural Obedience dog, but he is more than capable of learning and performing the exercises. These are relatively simple to begin with, involving heelwork, a recall and stays in the lowest class. As you progress, more exercises are added, and the aids you are allowed to give are reduced.

To achieve top honors in this discipline requires intensive training, as precision and accuracy are of paramount importance.

Agility

In this sport, the dog completes an obstacle course under the guidance of his owner. You need a good element of control, as the dog competes off the lead.

In competition, each dog completes the course individually and is assessed on both time and accuracy. The dog that completes the course in the fastest time, with the fewest faults, wins the class. The obstacles include an A-frame, a dog-walk, weaving poles, a seesaw, tunnels, and jumps.

There are different size categories, and, with lots of patience and positive training, the Pug can be an able competitor.

Showing

The Pug is a relatively easy breed to exhibit in the show ring as coat care is minimal. However, you need to spend time training your Pug to perform. A dog who does not like being handled by the judge, or one that does not walk smartly on the leash, is never going to win top honors, even if he is a top-quality animal.

To do well in the show ring, a Pug needs to enjoy himself so he shows the air of self-importance that is so typical of the breed. To prepare him for the busy show atmosphere, you need to work on his socialization, and then take him to ringcraft classes so you both learn what is required in the ring.

Showing at the top level is highly addictive, so watch out. Once you start, you will never have a free date in your diary!

Heelwork to music

Also known as Canine Freestyle, this activity is becoming increasingly popular. Dog and handler perform a choreographed routine to music, allowing the dog to show off an array of tricks and moves, which delight the crowd. The Pug has the out-going personality for this discipline, but there may be times when he takes the initiative and does a little Pug improvization!

Facing page:
In heelwork to music
dogs may be dressed to
look the part.

Health care

We are fortunate that a well-bred Pug, without exaggeration, is a healthy dog. With good routine care, a well-balanced diet, and sufficient exercise, most will experience few health problems and enjoy a good life expectancy.

However, it is your responsibility to put a program of preventative health care in place – and this should start from the moment your puppy, or older dog, arrives in his new home.

Vaccinations

Dogs are subject to a number of contagious diseases. In the old days, these were killers, and resulted in heartbreak for many owners. Vaccinations have now been developed, and the occurrence of the major infectious diseases is now very rare. However, this will only remain the case if all pet owners follow a strict policy of vaccinating their dogs.

There are vaccinations available for the following diseases:

Canine Adenovirus: This affects the liver; affected dogs have a classic 'blue eye'.

Distemper: A viral disease which causes chest and gastro-intestinal damage. The brain may also be affected, leading to fits and paralysis.

Parvovirus: Causes severe gastro enteritis, and most commonly affects puppies.

Leptospirosis: This bacterial disease is carried by rats and affects many mammals, including humans. It causes liver and kidney damage.

Rabies: A virus that affects the nervous system and is invariably fatal. The first signs are abnormal behavior when the infected dog may bite another animal or a person. Paralysis and death follow. Vaccination is compulsory in most countries. In the UK, dogs traveling overseas must be vaccinated.

Kennel Cough: There are several strains of Kennel Cough, but they all result in a harsh, dry, cough. This disease is rarely fatal; in fact most dogs make a good recovery within a matter of weeks and show few signs of ill health while they are affected. However, kennel cough is highly infectious among dogs that live together so, for this reason, most boarding kennels will insist that your dog is protected by the vaccine, which is given as nose drops.

Lyme Disease: This is a bacterial disease transmitted by ticks (see page 170). The first signs are limping, but the heart, kidneys and nervous system can also be affected. The ticks that transmit the disease occur in specific regions, such as the north-east states of the USA, some of the southern states, California and the upper Mississippi region. Lyme disease is still rare in the UK so vaccinations are not routinely offered.

Vaccination program

In the USA, the American Animal Hospital Association advises vaccination for core diseases, which they list as: distemper, adenovirus, parvovirus and rabies. The requirement for vaccinating for non-core diseases – leptospirosis, lyme disease and kennel cough – should be assessed depending on a dog's individual risk and his likely exposure to the disease.

In the UK, vaccinations are routinely given for distemper, adenovirus, leptospirosis and parvovirus.

In most cases, a puppy will start his vaccinations at around eight weeks of age, with the second part given a fortnight later. However, this does vary depending on the individual policy of your veterinary practice, and the incidence of disease in your area.

You should also talk to your vet about whether to give annual booster vaccinations. This depends on an individual dog's levels of immunity, and how long a particular vaccine remains effective.

Parasites

No matter how well you look after your Pug, you will have to accept that parasites – internal and external – are ever present, and you need to take preventative action.

Internal parasites: As the name suggests, these parasites live inside your dog. Most will find a home in the digestive tract, but there is also a parasite that lives in the heart. If infestation is unchecked, a dog's health will be severely jeopardized, but routine preventative treatment is simple and effective.

External parasites: These parasites live on your dog's body – in his skin and fur, and sometimes in his ears.

Roundworm

This is found in the small intestine, and signs of infestation will be a poor coat, a pot belly, diarrhoea and lethargy. Pregnant mothers should be treated, but it is almost inevitable that parasites will be passed on to the puppies. For this reason, a breeder will start a worming program, which you will need to continue. Ask your vet for advice on treatment, which will need to continue throughout your dog's life.

Tapeworm

Infection occurs when fleas and lice are ingested; the adult worm takes up residence in the small intestine, releasing mobile segments (which contain eggs) which can be seen in a dog's feces as small rice-like grains. The only other obvious sign of infestation is irritation of the anus. Again, routine preventative treatment is required throughout your Pug's life.

Heartworm

This parasite is transmitted by mosquitoes, and so will only occur where these insects thrive. A warm environment is needed for the parasite to develop, so it is more likely to be present in areas with a warm, humid climate. However, it is found in all parts of the USA, although its prevalence does vary. At present, heartworm is rarely seen in the UK.

Heartworm live in the right side of the heart. Larvae can grow up to 14in (35.5cm) in length. A dog with heartworm is at severe risk from heart failure, so preventative treatment, as advised by your vet, is essential. Dogs living in the USA should have regular blood tests to check for the presence of infection.

Lungworm

Lungworm is a parasite that lives in the heart and major blood vessels supplying the lungs. It can cause many problems, such as breathing difficulties, blood-clotting problems, sickness and diarrhoea, seizures, and can even be fatal. The parasite is carried by slugs and snails, and the dog becomes infected when ingesting these, often accidentally when rummaging through undergrowth. Lungworm is not common, but it is on the increase and a responsible owner should be aware of it. Fortunately, it is easily preventable and even affected dogs usually make a full recovery if treated early enough. Your vet will be able to advise you on the risks in your area and what form of treatment may be required.

Fleas

A dog may carry dog fleas, cat fleas, and even human fleas. The flea stays on the dog only long enough to have a blood meal and to breed, but its presence will result in itching and scratching. If your dog has an

allergy to fleas – which is usually a reaction to the flea's saliva – he will scratch himself until he is raw.

Spot-on treatment, which should be administered on a routine basis, is easy to use and highly effective on all types of fleas. You can also treat your dog with a spray or with insecticidal shampoo. Bear in mind that the whole environment your dog lives in will need to be sprayed, and all other pets living in your home will also need to be treated.

How to detect fleas

You may suspect your dog has fleas, but how can you be sure? There are two methods to try.

Run a fine comb through your dog's coat, and see if you can detect the presence of fleas on the skin, or clinging to the comb. Alternatively, sit your dog on some white paper and rub his back. This will dislodge feces from the fleas, which will be visible as small brown specks. To double check, shake the specks on to some damp cotton (cotton-wool). Flea feces consists of the dried blood taken from the host, so if the specks turn a lighter shade of red, you know your dog has fleas.

Ticks

These are blood-sucking parasites which are most frequently found in rural area where sheep or deer are present. The main danger is their ability to pass lyme disease to both dogs and humans. Lyme disease is prevalent in some areas of the USA (see page 163), although it is still rare in the UK. The treatment you give your dog for fleas generally works for ticks, but you should discuss the best product to use with your vet.

How to remove a tick

If you spot a tick on your dog, do not try to pluck it off as you risk leaving the hard mouth parts embedded in his skin. The best way to remove a tick is to use a fine pair of tweezers or you can buy a tick remover. Grasp the tick head firmly and then pull the tick straight out from the skin. If you are using a tick remover, check the instructions, as some recommend a circular twist when pulling. When you have removed the tick, clean the area with mild soap and water.

Ear mites

These parasites live in the outer ear canal. The signs of infestation are a brown, waxy discharge, and your dog will continually shake his head and scratch his ear. If you suspect your Pug has ear mites, a visit to the vet will be needed so that medicated ear drops can be prescribed.

Fur mites

These small, white parasites are visible to the naked eye and are often referred to as 'walking dandruff'. They cause a scurfy coat and mild itchiness. However, they are zoonetic – transferable to humans – so prompt treatment with an insecticide prescribed by your vet is essential.

Harvest mites

These are picked up from the undergrowth, and can be seen as a bright orange patch on the webbing between the toes, although this can be found elsewhere on the body, such as the ear flaps. Treatment is effective with the appropriate insecticide.

Skin mites

There are two types of parasite that burrow into a dog's skin. *Demodex canis* is transferred from a mother to her pups while they are feeding. Treatment is with a topical preparation, and sometimes antibiotics are needed.

The other skin mite, *Sarcoptes scabiei*, causes intense itching and hair loss. It is highly contagious, so all dogs in a household will need to be treated, which involves repeated bathing with a medicated shampoo.

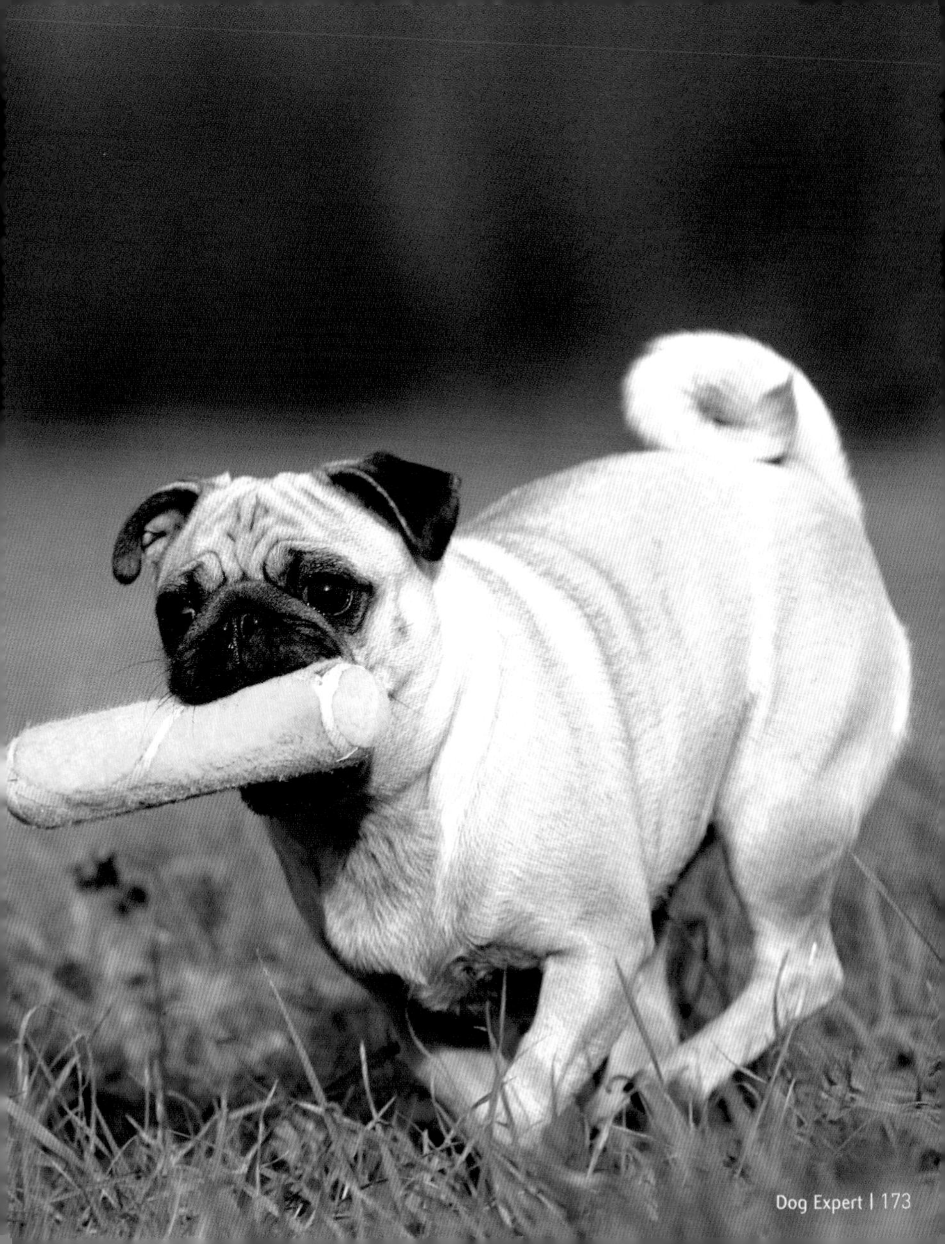

Common
ailments

As with all living animals, dogs can be affected by a variety of ailments. Most can be treated effectively after consulting with your vet, who will prescribe appropriate medication and will advise you on how to meet your dog's needs. Here are some of the more common problems that could affect your Pug, with advice on how to deal with them.

Anal glands

These are two small sacs on either side of the anus, which produce a dark-brown secretion that dogs use when they mark their territory. The anal glands should empty every time a dog defecates but if they become blocked or impacted, a dog will experience increasing discomfort. He may nibble at his rear end, or 'scoot' his bottom along the ground to relieve the irritation. Treatment involves a trip to the vet, who

will empty the glands manually. It is important to do this without delay or infection may occur.

Dental problems

The incidence of dental problems has increased dramatically in recent times and, as highlighted earlier, good dental hygiene will do much to minimize problems with gum infection and tooth decay. If tartar accumulates to the extent that you cannot remove it by brushing, the vet will need to intervene. In a situation such as this, an anesthetic will need to be administered so the tartar can be removed manually.

Diarrhoea

There are many reasons why a dog has diarrhoea, but most commonly it is the result of scavenging, a sudden change of diet, or an adverse reaction to a particular type of food.

If your dog is suffering from diarrhoea, the first step is to withdraw food for a day. It is important that he does not dehydrate, so make sure that fresh drinking water is available. However, drinking too much can increase the diarrhoea, which may be accompanied with vomiting, so limit how much he drinks at any one time.

After allowing the stomach to rest, feed a bland diet, such as white fish or chicken with boiled rice, for a few days. In most cases, your dog's motions will return to normal and you can resume normal feeding, although this should be done gradually.

However, if this fails to work and the diarrhoea persists for more than a few days, you should consult you vet. Your dog may have an infection which needs to be treated with antibiotics, or the diarrhoea may indicate some other problem which needs expert diagnosis.

Ear infections

The Pug has rose or button ears, so air will not circulate as easily as it does in dogs with semi-pricked or pricked ears. This means that a Pug may be prone to ear infections.

A healthy ear is clean with no sign of redness or inflammation, and no evidence of a waxy brown discharge or a foul odor. If you see your dog scratching his ear, shaking his head, or holding one ear at an odd angle, you will need to consult your vet.

The most likely causes are ear mites, an infection, or there may a foreign body, such as a grass seed, trapped in the ear. Depending on the cause, treatment is with medicated ear drops, possibly containing antibiotics. If a foreign body is suspected, the vet will need to carry our further investigations.

Eye problems

The Pug has large, round eyes, and while the eyeballs should not protrude, they are more vulnerable than in other breeds. It is not unusual for the eye to be injured by a thorn, or some other sharp object, so take care where you exercise your dog.

If your Pug's eyes look red and sore, he may be suffering from conjunctivitis. This may, or may not, be accompanied with a watery or a crusty discharge.

Conjunctivitis can be caused by a bacterial or viral infection, it could be the result of an injury, or it could be an adverse reaction to pollen.

You will need to consult your vet for a correct diagnosis, but in the case of an infection, treatment with medicated eye drops is effective.

Conjunctivitis may also be the first sign of more serious inherited eye problems (see page 186).

In some instances, your dog may suffer from dry, itchy eye, which he may further injure through scratching. This condition, known as *keratoconjunctivitis sicca*, may be inherited (see page 187).

Foreign bodies

In the home, puppies – and some older dogs – cannot resist chewing anything that looks interesting. The toys you choose for your dog should be suitably robust to withstand damage, but children's toys can be irresistible. Some dogs will chew – and swallow – anything from socks, tights, and any other items from the laundry basket, to golf balls and stones from the garden. Obviously, these items are indigestible and could cause an obstruction in your dog's intestine, which is potentially lethal.

The signs to look for are vomiting, and a tucked up

posture. The dog will often be restless and will look as though he is in pain.

In this situation, you must get your dog to the vet without delay as surgery will be needed to remove the obstruction.

Heatstroke

The Pug is one of the brachycephalic dog breeds, which include the Pekingese, the Bulldog, the French Bulldog and the Lhasa Apso. All these dogs have a shorter muzzle than most other breeds, and a flatter nose. Although this feature should not be exaggerated, it does mean that these breeds may have more labored breathing and, as a result, they will overheat more easily. This can result in a condition known as Brachycephalic Upper Airway Syndrome (see page 186).

On hot days, make sure your dog always has access to shady areas, and wait for a cooler part of the day before going for a walk. Be extra careful if you leave your Pug in the car, as the temperature can rise dramatically – even on a cloudy day. Heatstroke can happen very rapidly, and unless you are able lower your dog's temperature, it can be fatal.

If your Pug appears to be suffering from heatstroke, lie him flat and try to reduce his core body temperature by wrapping him in cool towels. A dog should not be immersed in cold water as this will cause the blood vessels to constrict, impeding heat dissipation. As soon as he has made some recovery, take him to the vet, where cold intravenous fluids can be administered.

Lameness/limping

There are a wide variety of reasons why a dog can go lame – from a simple muscle strain, to a fracture, ligament damage, or more complex problems with the joints. If you are concerned about your dog, do not delay in seeking help.

As your Pug becomes more elderly, he may suffer from arthritis, which you will see as general stiffness, particularly when he gets up after resting. It will help if you ensure his bed is in a warm, draft-free location, and if your Pug gets wet after exercise, you must dry him thoroughly.

If your Pug seems to be in pain, consult your vet who will be able to help with pain relief medication.

Skin problems

If your dog is scratching or nibbling at his skin, first check he is free from fleas (see page 168). There are other external parasites that cause itching and hair loss, but you will need a vet to help you find the culprit.

An allergic reaction is another major cause of skin problems. It can be quite an undertaking to find the cause of the allergy, and you will need to follow your vet's advice, which often requires eliminating specific ingredients from the diet, as well as looking at environmental factors.

Inherited disorders

There are a number of conditions that can be passed on from one generation to the next, and there are some disorders that a particular breed will be more likely to inherit. Although Pug breeders strive to eliminate these problems from their bloodlines, it is important to research thoroughly before buying a puppy.

Brachycephalic upper airway syndrome

This condition affects brachycephalic breeds because of the way they are constructed. The foreshortened muzzle and flattened nose, combined with an overlong soft palate, can cause difficulty in breathing. This is most evident in hot and humid weather, and so great care should be taken to ensure that the Pug does not over-exert himself in these conditions.

Collapsing trachea

This is caused by a malformation of the windpipe, causing the airway to collapse and restricting airflow into the lungs.

It is often characterized by a honking cough, and is more evident when a Pug is excited, or when he is pulling against his collar. In some cases, a Pug may cough when he tries to eat or drink.

Treatment is needed to suppress the cough and inflammation. Using a harness rather than a collar is also recommended.

Eye conditions

The Pug is predisposed to a couple of inherited eye conditions, and some are due to the structure of his skull. As highlighted earlier, brachycephalic breeds have a foreshortened muzzle; they also have shallow eye sockets, which makes the eyes more prominent. In some dogs, this can result in an inability to close both eyelids over the eye. This can cause a condition known as exposure keratitis, which results in inflammation and ulceration of the cornea.

The Pug can also suffer from *keratoconjunctivitis sicca*, also known as dry eye. This is caused by inadequate tear production, which can result in clouding of the cornea and eventual loss of vision. The most effective treatment is using tear substitutes to lubricate the eyes, or drugs to stimulate tear production.

Entropion is an inherited condition in Pugs and involves the in-turning of the eyelids, which means that the eyeball is often irritated by in-growing eyelashes. Surgical correction is generally successful.

Hemivertebrae

This is where the vertebrae of the spine are mis-shapen so they cannot perform their role of protecting the spinal cord. The impact of the disease varies depending on the extent of the deformity, but it may result in paralysis. In some cases, surgery may be successful.

Legge perthes disease

This is a condition where the ball of the thigh bone dies before the skeleton matures, resulting in pain and lameness. It is generally seen in puppies aged four to six months. Early diagnosis, rest and pain relief may help, but surgery is often recommended.

Patellar luxation

The kneecap (patella) slips out of place, causing the knee or stifle to lock so that it is unable to bend. The characteristic sign is when a Pug hops for a few paces, and then resumes his normal gait when the patella slips back into position.

Surgery may be needed in severe cases but generally a Pug will live with this condition and be largely unaffected, although arthritis may occur in the stifle in later life.

Pug dog encephalitis

This is a rare condition, involving inflammation of the brain, which is only diagnosed on post mortem examination. An affected Pug may suffer loss of vision and fits; coma and death may follow in a few days or weeks.

Generally, the onset of this disease is from six months, but dogs as old as seven have appeared healthy and then fallen victim to the disease.

As there is no means of diagnosing the disease, there is the possibility that affected dogs may be bred from, making it very difficult to eliminate from breeding programs.

Summing up

It may give the pet owner cause for concern to find about health problems that may affect their Pug. But it is important to bear in mind that acquiring some basic knowledge is an asset, as it will allow you to spot signs of trouble at an early stage. Early diagnosis is very often the means to the most effective treatment.

Fortunately, the Pug is generally a healthy and disease-free dog with his only visits to the vet being annual check-ups. In most cases, owners can look forward to enjoying many happy years with this affectionate and highly entertaining companion.

Useful addresses

Breed & Kennel Clubs

Please contact your Kennel Club to obtain contact information about breed clubs in your area.

UK

The Kennel Club (UK)
1 Clarges Street London, W1J 8AB
Telephone: 0870 606 6750
Fax: 0207 518 1058
Web: www.thekennelclub.org.uk

USA

American Kennel Club (AKC)
5580 Centerview Drive, Raleigh, NC 27606.
Telephone: 919 233 9767
Fax: 919 233 3627
Email: info@akc.org
Web: www.akc.org

United Kennel Club (UKC)
100 E Kilgore Rd, Kalamazoo,
MI 49002-5584, USA.
Tel: 269 343 9020
Fax: 269 343 7037
Web:www.ukcdogs.com/

Australia

Australian National Kennel Council (ANKC)
The Australian National Kennel Council is the administrative body for pure breed canine affairs in Australia. It does not, however, deal directly with dog exhibitors, breeders or judges. For information pertaining to breeders, clubs or shows, please contact the relevant State or Territory Body.

International

Fédération Cynologique Internationalé (FCI)
Place Albert 1er, 13, B-6530 Thuin, Belgium.
Tel: +32 71 59.12.38
Fax: +32 71 59.22.29
Web: www.fci.be/

Training and behavior

UK

Association of Pet Dog Trainers
Telephone: 01285 810811
Web: http://www.apdt.co.uk

Canine Behaviour
Association of Pet Behaviour Counsellors
Telephone: 01386 751151
Web: http://www.apbc.org.uk/

USA

Association of Pet Dog Trainers
Tel: 1 800 738 3647
Web: www.apdt.com/

American College of Veterinary Behaviorists
Web: http://dacvb.org/

American Veterinary Society of Animal Behavior
Web: www.avsabonline.org/

Australia

APDT Australia Inc
Web: www.apdt.com.au

For details of regional behaviorists, contact the relevant State or Territory Controlling Body.

Activities

UK

Agility Club
http://www.agilityclub.co.uk/

British Flyball Association
Telephone: 01628 829623
Web: http://www.flyball.org.uk/

USA

North American Dog Agility Council
Web: www.nadac.com/

North American Flyball Association, Inc.
Tel/Fax: 800 318 6312
Web: www.flyball.org/

Australia

Agility Dog Association of Australia
Tel: 0423 138 914
Web: www.adaa.com.au/

NADAC Australia
Web: www.nadacaustralia.com/

Australian Flyball Association
Tel: 0407 337 939
Web: www.flyball.org.au/

International

World Canine Freestyle Organisation
Tel: (718) 332-8336
Web: www.worldcaninefreestyle.org

Health

UK

British Small Animal Veterinary Association
Tel: 01452 726700
Web: http://www.bsava.com/

Royal College of Veterinary Surgeons
Tel: 0207 222 2001
Web: www.rcvs.org.uk

www.dogbooksonline.co.uk/healthcare/

Alternative Veterinary Medicine Centre
Tel: 01367 710324
Web: www.alternativevet.org/

USA

American Veterinary Medical Association
Tel: 800 248 2862
Web: www.avma.org

American College of Veterinary Surgeons
Tel: 301 916 0200
Toll Free: 877 217 2287
Web: www.acvs.org/

Canine Eye Registration Foundation
The Veterinary Medical DataBases
1717 Philo Rd, PO Box 3007,
Urbana, IL 61803-3007
Tel: 217-693-4800
Fax: 217-693-4801
Web: http://www.vmdb.org/cerf.html

Orthopedic Foundation of Animals
2300 E Nifong Boulevard
Columbia, Missouri, 65201-3806
Tel: 573 442-0418
Fax: 573 875-5073
Web: http://www.offa.org/

American Holistic Veterinary Medical
Association
Tel: 410 569 0795
Web: www.ahvma.org/

Australia

Australian Small Animal Veterinary
Association
Tel: 02 9431 5090
Web: www.asava.com.au

Australian Veterinary Association
Tel: 02 9431 5000
Web: www.ava.com.au

Australian College Veterinary Scientists
Tel: 07 3423 2016
Web: http://acvsc.org.au

Australian Holistic Vets
Web: www.ahv.com.au/